The Joke Book
For People Who Think Getting Old
Is a Joke

"Finally, baby boomers and old people have something to laugh about..."

The Joke Book For People Who Think Getting Old Is a Joke

by The Unknown Comic

BearManor Media
2015

The Joke Book For People Who Think Getting Old Is a Joke
© 2015 Murray Langston

All rights reserved.

For information, address:

BearManor Media
P. O. Box 71426
Albany, GA 31708

bearmanormedia.com

Typesetting and layout by John Teehan

Published in the USA by BearManor Media

ISBN—1-59393-783-0
978-1-59393-783-6

Contents

Part 1	You Know You're Getting Old…............	1
Part 2	You Know You're "Already" Too Old…................................	7
Part 3	MEN ONLY – You Know You're Too Old…....................	11
Part 4	WOMEN ONLY – You Know You're Too Old…......................	15
Part 5	Remember the Old Days…................	19
Part 6	Old "Quotes"…..............................	23
Part 7	Celebrity "Quotes"….......................	27
Part 8	For All You Young People….............	29
Part 9	Old "Thoughts"…..........................	31
Part 10	Getting "OLD" is a Bitch….............	33

Part 11	Good Things About Getting "OLD"... 39
Part 12	Overheard In a Retirement Home... 43
Part 13	The World's BEST "OLD" JOKES.. 49
Part 14	Life Is Really Wonderful...................... 79

Part 1

You Know You're Getting Old...

If foreplay is a nudge.

If getting up… gets you down.

If you only listen to talk radio.

If you carry around a change purse.

If a quickie before dinner is a Martini.

If you think 'N Sync is a drain cleaner.

If your back goes out… more than you do.

If your get up and go has got up and gone.

If sex is more of a memory than a passion.

If your childhood toys are now in a museum.

If you own more than one medical dictionary.

If there's nothing left to learn the hard way.

If people call at 9 p.m. and ask, "Did I wake you?"

If the only drugs you now take are prescription.

If you no longer think amusement parks are fun.

If your baby pictures are only in black and white.

If you look exactly like your driver's license picture.

If the pharmacist has become your new best friend.

If you find yourself listening to your children's advice.

If you find yourself singing along with elevator music.

If "Howdy Doody" means a successful bowel movement!

If in the middle of having sex you forget where you are.

If you sink your teeth into a steak… and they stay there.

If everything hurts, and what doesn't hurt doesn't work.

If caution is the only thing left that you care to exercise.

If you no longer set bad examples but start giving good advice.

If you give up all your bad habits… and still don't feel good.

If the only time you cheat on your spouse… is during Scrabble.

If the candles on your birthday cake cost more than the cake.

If you think the best way to start a day… is to stay in bed.

If you want to be nostalgic… but you can't remember anything.

If you can still do as much as you did before… but you don't.

If whenever you eat soup in a restaurant, people get up and dance.

If you can finally sleep in… but you still get up every morning at six.

If you want your sex drive lowered… because now it's all in your head.

If you walk into an antique store… and two people try to buy you.

If you can remember when Baskin & Robbins had two flavors.

If "tying one on"… means fastening your medic-alert bracelet.

If the last time you went jogging you got arrested for Loitering.

If you finally get your shit together… then realize you can't lift it.

If you have all your Christmas cards mailed by the end of November.

If your idea of an exciting night in bed… is turning up the electric blanket.

If you have to recite the entire alphabet to remember where one letter is?

If you're told to slow down more often by your doctor than by the police.

If you get up feeling bad… without having had fun the night before.

If you take up jogging… mainly so you can hear heavy breathing again.

If you're masturbating and you forget who you were fantasizing about.

If you don't care how long you stay out… as long as you're home by nine.

If the first thing you do when you get up in the morning is take a nap.

If your friends compliment you on your new alligator shoes and you're barefoot.

If you're feeling your oats a lot less… and feeling your corns a lot more.

If every time you feel like exercising, you lie down until that feeling goes away.

If you start turning the lights out for economic reasons rather than romantic reasons.

If the clothes you put away until they come back in style… have come back in style.

If you've stopped growing at both ends and are now growing in the middle.

If you can remember having to walk across the room to turn your TV on.

If the first time you tried snorting coke… you got the bottle stuck up your nose.

If you've come to the annoying realization that your parents were right about everything.

If you have a choice of two temptations… and you choose the one that will get you home earlier.

If the only thing you want for your birthday… is to not be reminded of it.

If opportunity knocks, but you're too tired to get up and answer the door.

If you have so many liver spots, vegetarians refuse to shake hands with you.

If you used to avoid temptation… and now realize that temptation avoids you.

If you can remember saying, "Get off the internet… I need to use the phone…"

If instead of looking forward to owning a BMW… you now look forward to having a BM.

If you are no longer as interested in the Rolling Stones as you are in your kidney stones.

If that squeak you thought was coming from your shoe… was actually coming from your knee.

If you don't do drugs anymore because you can get the same effect just by standing up real fast.

If you walk into a room and suddenly can't remember why you went in there… and you're in the toilet.

If someone asks you if you remember the first time you had sex, and you reply, "I can't remember the last time I had sex."

If you can remember where you were when President Kennedy was shot, but can't remember where you put your car keys.

If you take a vacation to forget everything, then when you get there, you open your suitcase and find that you forgot everything.

If you used to be able to drink all weekend and feel okay… but today, after a weekend of drinking, you usually require some minor surgery.

If you can remember your Social Security number, your driver's license number, your area code, and your bank account number, but you can't remember which is which.

Part 2

You Know You're "Already" Too Old...

If you begin collecting "dust."

If you get winded playing chess.

If your grandkids… have grandkids.

If you don't get any of these jokes.

If you no longer update your resumé.

If your rocking chair has a seatbelt.

If you like to take naps during sex.

If your social security number is… 9.

If you frequently fall asleep mid-sentence.

If undertakers are sending you estimates.

If you occasionally forget your own name.

If your children no longer let you use scissors.

If you masturbate… and your hand falls asleep.

If you realize you no longer have peer pressure.

If you get congratulated when you get out of bed.

If you remember when the Dead Sea was only sick.

If someone tells you to act your age… and you die.

If you sit in a rocking chair and can't get it started.

If you no longer have enemies because they're all dead.

If, on your last birthday, your family got you a new bedpan.

If you get married and Medicare pays for your honeymoon.

If you get married and spend your honeymoon getting out of the car.

If a threesome for you… is two people helping you get out of bed.

If you have to ask where the bathroom is… and you're in your own home.

If you eat nothing but junk food, hoping to get as many preservatives as you can.

If you can't remember who was president the last time you had sex.

If it is no longer possible for your friends to drink to your health.

If you take a nap and everyone becomes worried you might be dead.

If you go to your eye doctor and he tells you that your contacts have cataracts.

If you stop playing golf because you don't want to get close to a hole in the ground.

If your memory is getting so bad… you can plan your own surprise party.

If, on your birthday, people say, "You look great for your age… almost life like."

If you still think you're a sex symbol, but are not sure which sex you're a symbol of.

If you can't sunbathe for longer than ten minutes because vultures start blocking out the sun.

If your doctor doesn't give you x-rays anymore, but just holds <u>you</u> up to the light.

If your five-year-old grandson likes you to take him to the bathroom because your hands shake.

If you always place your hand in front of your mouth before you sneeze… to catch your teeth.

If you go for a short walk… and three days later, the cops return you to your house.

If your insurance policy used to cover you for injury during an Native-American raid.

If at dinner you're asked to pass the salt and pepper… and you have to make two trips.

If you need a fire permit to light the candles on your birthday cake.

If while you're thinking about taking a nap… you fall asleep for twenty minutes.

If you can only blow out the candles on your birthday cake one at a time.

If they light the candles on your birthday cake… and fourteen people are overcome by the smoke.

If you've seen it all and done it all… but you can't remember any of it.

If you can remember going to the movies when Walter Brennan got the girl.

If you frequently check the newspaper to see if your name is in the obituary column.

If you don't laugh out loud anymore because you're afraid your teeth might fly out.

If the last time someone kissed you was to give you mouth to mouth resuscitation.

If when you were in the first grade, you could name all the Presidents easily because there were only four of them.

If you have a habit of pretending you're deaf because you think you've already heard everything that's worth hearing.

If you go horseback riding every day except Thursday, because Thursday is the day the man who puts you on the horse has the day off.

If you have so many wrinkles on your body that when you shower, it takes over twenty minutes for the water to drain down your body.

If you think back on your life and you realize that if you had to do it all over again you'd make the same mistakes but you would start sooner.

Part 3

– MEN ONLY –
You Know You're Too Old...

If you never trust a fart.

If you never pass a toilet.

If you never waste an erection.

If you fake premature ejaculations.

If ALL women now look good to you.

If you can't take "Yes" for an answer.

If you take a bath... and your balls float.

If your knees buckle, but your belt won't.

If your idea of weight lifting is standing up.

If you still chase women... but only downhill.

If young women begin opening doors for you.

If you no longer need a pillow to play Santa Claus.

If you can braid the hair growing out of your nose.

If you know where it's at but forget why it's there.

If your memory is the second thing that's getting shorter.

If instead of growing pot, you're growing a pot belly.

If you have an orgasm and a puff of dust comes out.

If "getting lucky" means finding your car in the parking lot.

If the little old lady you help cross the street… is your wife.

If when you have sex, you don't orgasm until a week later.

If you realize you're too old to be a member of a boy band.

If not only is your age creeping up on you but so is your underwear.

If you no longer have a zip in your step… but a jiggle in your belly.

If your fantasy of two women is one washing and one cleaning.

If all the numbers in your little black book are doctors' numbers.

If someone asks if you wear boxers or briefs and you reply, "Depends."

If seeing a beautiful woman arouses your memory instead of your hopes.

If you have sex with a prostitute, and afterward she gives you a refund.

If a sexy babe catches your fancy and your pacemaker opens the garage door.

If you don't care where your spouse goes, just as long as you don't have to go along.

If you've stopped worrying about hair loss and have started worrying about memory loss.

If every time you pass a bathroom, you think, "I may as well pee while I'm here."

If you've quit trying to hold your stomach in, no matter who walks into the room.

If you no longer want a threesome so you don't have to worry about disappointing two people.

If you have a choice between sex and a bowel movement… and you head for the toilet.

If an all-nighter used to mean partying all night, now it means not having to get up to pee.

If you want to apologize to your wife for an argument you had but can't remember what it was about.

If you drop something on the ground and decide to wait until you have to tie your shoelaces before picking it up.

If your wife says, "Let's go upstairs and make love," and you answer, "Honey, you know I can't do both!"

- If, for you, taking Viagra is like putting a brand new flag pole… on a condemned building.

- If you go on a date and she says, "You're only interested in one thing."… And you can't remember what it is.

- If you and your wife get a hotel room with a mirror over the bed… and you use it to shave.

- If you're losing hair where you want it… and growing hair where you don't want it.

- If the number of times you get up to pee exceeds the number of hours you sleep.

- If the only thing you have in common with a soccer player is that you can both hit your balls with your knees.

- If you forget names, then you forget faces, then you forget to pull up your zipper, and, worse, you forget to pull it down.

Part 4

– WOMEN ONLY –
You Know You're Too Old...

If you scare small children.

If your skin is naturally curly.

If your favorite movie star is Gabby Hayes.

If you think a mini pad is a small apartment.

If exercise for you is taking three laxatives.

If it takes you twice as long to look half as good.

If you can't remember your own children's names.

If "getting lucky" is someone else doing the dishes.

If, for sex, instead of Vaseline you prefer Polygrip.

If you're approaching middle age for the third time.

If your breast size has gone from a 34C to a 38 long.

If going bra-less pulls all the wrinkles out of your face.

If a two-pound box of candy… makes you gain ten pounds.

If Mick Jagger and Paul McCartney don't look old to you.

If you used to wine and dine, but now you just dine and wine.

If your favorite time to work on a crossword puzzle… is during sex.

If you are frequently asked if you've been marinating in perfume.

If you give your marriage one more try for the sake of the parakeet.

If you finally get your head together… and your body falls apart.

If you can remember when birth control was pretending to be asleep.

If you're lounging by the pool and people dress you with their eyes.

If you worry more about how your shoe fits than how your bikini fits.

If you've gone from having a cute vagina… to having acute angina.

If that little tumor between your breasts… turns out to be your navel.

If a man kisses your neck and his teeth get caught in your wrinkles.

If you buy a new bathing suit… because your old one has a hole at the knee.

If after sex, your lover gives you flowers… because he thinks you're dead.

If the only time you get sexually aroused is when you hear the word, "Bingo."

If you have so many wrinkles on your forehead, you have to screw your hat on.

If you decide to marry someone you wouldn't have talked to twenty years before.

If your husband tells you that your nylons are wrinkled… and you're not wearing any.

If you like mosquitoes… because they're the only things left that want you for your body.

If you have a hard time not only remembering your first kiss but also your first husband.

If you can remember when birth control was crossing your legs or crossing your fingers.

If your secrets are safe with your friends because they either can't remember them or are dead.

If you refuse to wear earrings because you have so many wrinkles it makes you look like venetian blinds.

If you greet your husband naked when he comes home from work… and he tells you that your dress needs ironing.

Part 5

Remember the Old Days...

Remember when we were young and couldn't wait to grow up... What the hell were we thinking...?

* * *

Still, I feel sorry for young people who aren't old enough to remember the good old days.

* * *

– Times have Changed –

Remember when you could carry the Sunday paper in one hand?

Remember when politicians were looked up to and not looked into?

Remember when children had more brothers and sisters than mothers and fathers?

Remember when we didn't drink water from a bottle... we drank water from a garden hose?

* * *

When I was a kid, I hated broccoli and I hated getting spanked. Now I love broccoli, and getting spanked ain't bad either.

* * *

Remember the old days when you had long hair? Nowadays you long for hair.

Remember the old days when you used to look for killer weed? Nowadays, you look for weed killer.

Remember the old days when women used to cook like their mothers? Nowadays, they drink like their fathers.

Remember the old days when you could make love all night long? Nowadays, you long to make love for just one night.

Remember the old days when you could open your window and listen to birds singing? Nowadays you open your window and listen to birds coughing.

Remember the old days, when a man courted a girl for six months, then married her? Nowadays, a man marries a girl, then in six months they go to court.

Remember the old days, when kids played doctor by examining each other? Nowadays when kids play doctor, one operates… and the other sues.

Remember the old days, when you looked forward to going out to a new hip joint? Nowadays, your doctor tells you that you *need* a new hip joint.

Remember the old days, when a couple would postpone their wedding because they couldn't find a church? Nowadays, a couple will postpone their wedding because they can't find a babysitter.

Remember the old days when you would walk into a kitchen and say, "What's cooking?" Nowadays, you walk into a kitchen and say, "What's thawing?"

Remember the old days, when a man asked a woman to marry him, he'd get on his knees and say, "Darling, will you marry me?" Nowadays, when a man asks a girl to marry him, he says, "Hey, how'd you like to do this every night?"

Part 6

Wise Old "Quotes"

"I'm not old… I just need some WD-40."

"The real secret to youth… is lying about it."

"He who dies with the most toys… still dies."

"Age is a very high price to pay for maturity."

"Growing old is inevitable… growing up is optional."

"You're never too old to learn new ways… to be stupid."

"Time may be a great healer… but it's a lousy beautician."

"Age doesn't always bring wisdom. Sometimes age comes alone."

"If you can remember the '60s… You weren't really there."

"Make sure you take care of your life. Without it, you'd be dead."

"A man is only as old as he looks… and if he only looks… he's old."

"Wrinkled was not one of the things I wanted to be when I grew up."

"Last will and testament: Being of sound mind… I spent all my money."

"The only good thing about old age… is that you only go through it once."

"It's not the good old days that I miss… it's those good old nights."

"Be nice to your friends. One day you may need them to change your bedpan."

"Now that I've finally learned to make the most of life… Most of it's gone."

"You don't stop laughing when you grow old… You grow old when you stop laughing."

"Life begins at forty… and so does arthritis, rheumatism, and prostate problems."

"Sure, life begins at forty… but if you wait that long… you'll miss out on a lot."

"I really don't know that much about growing old because I've never done it before."

"I'm getting really close to becoming one of those senior citizens who bites everyone."

"The old believe everything. The middle aged suspect everything. The young know everything."

"Middle age people have money and energy but no time. Old people have time and money but no energy."

"I'm finally old enough where I don't care what people say about me and now nobody says anything."

"I really don't mind those senior moments… it's those senior hours that confuse the crap out of me."

"When I was a kid I wanted to be older… but now that I'm here, this shit isn't what I expected at all."

"If it weren't for miracle drugs… people wouldn't be able to live long enough to pay their medical bills."

Part 7

Celebrity Quotes

"I've outlived my dick..." – *Willie Nelson*

"So far, this is the oldest I've been." – *George Carlin*

"I intend to live forever. So far, so good." – *Steven Wright*

"A man's only as old as the woman he feels." – *Groucho Marx*

"Being healthy is basically dying as slowly as possible." – *Ricky Gervais*

"I respect old age… especially when it's bottled." – *Dean Martin*

"Sex after sixty… is like trying to shoot pool with a rope." – *Redd Foxx*

"The best form of birth control after sixty is nudity." – *Phyllis Diller*

"In the end it's not the years in a life, it's the life in the years." – *Abe Lincoln*

"Time may be a great healer… but plastic surgery is quicker." – *Joan Rivers*

"Tomorrow I'll be celebrating my ninetieth birthday. How?… I don't know." – *George Burns*

"Though I'm in my sixties… I have nothing in common with adults." – *Murray Langston*

"Rather than growing old gracefully, I'd prefer growing old disgracefully. – *Pat Paulsen*

"When I die, I want my grave to have free Wi-Fi so people will come visit more often." – *Unknown*

"Life is like a roll of toilet paper. The closer it gets to the end, the faster it goes." – *Andy Rooney*

"I've discovered that even in my eighties, when it comes to sex, you're never too old to yearn." – *Bob Hope*

"To some people, men look distinguished with grey hair. To me, they look like they ran out of dye." – *Dom DeLuise*

"I'm going to start telling people that I'm ten years older than I am… so they can tell me how good I look for my age." – *Ruth Buzzi*

Part 8

For All You Young People...

Don't grow up… it's a trap…

Don't worry about old age… it doesn't last that long.

Never complain about the coffee… You may be old and weak someday.

It's a shame that by the time most young people realize how much fun it is to be young… they're old.

Part 9

"OLD" Thoughts...

Age is important… only if you're cheese.

If the good die young… are all old people bad?

A perfect older couple is when he snores and she's deaf.

A woman is just as beautiful at forty as she is at twenty… it just takes longer.

Have you noticed that the future keeps getting closer and closer and closer?

One way to live longer… is to cut out all the things that make you want to live longer.

The reason older people read the Bible more than younger people… is because they're cramming for their finals.

Now that I'm older, I thought it was great that I seemed to have more patience… turns out I just don't give a shit.

Part 10

GETTNG OLD Is a Bitch...

Inside every older person is a younger person wondering... "What the fuck happened?"

* * *

As soon as you get old enough to know better... you realize you don't know shit.

* * *

Today, I was at the eye doctor... He asked me to read the third line on the chart... I said, "What chart?"

* * *

The number one sign for dementia... is when you google the warning signs for dementia.

* * *

I found out last night that the only thing worse than getting up twice to pee... is sleeping through it.

* * *

Before I got married, my wife always said, "You're only interested in one thing." Now I can't remember what it was.

* * *

A ninety-two-year-old grandmother tried dying her hair but it turned out lousy... Apparently, only the young "dye" good.

* * *

It's a bitch getting old when you're driving, and you speed up to get where you're going before you forget where you're going.

* * *

Now in my sixties I enjoy Social Security sex... "When you get a little every month, but it's not really enough to live on."

* * *

I went to my fortieth class reunion. What a waste. All of my old classmates were so old, fat, and bald that none of them recognized me.

* * *

What a rip off. I went to a bar that offered free drinks to anyone sixty-five or older. When I got there, I found out you had to bring both your parents.

* * *

The first things to go when a man gets old are his knees.

First his "right knee," then his "left knee," then his "kid nee," then his "hi nee," and finally his "wee nee."

* * *

Sure I've gotten old. I've had two bypass surgeries, a hip replacement, new knees, fought prostate cancer, and diabetes. I'm half blind, can't hear much, take twenty different medications that make me dizzy, winded, and subject to blackouts. I have bouts with dementia, poor circulation, hardly feel my hands and feet anymore, can't remember if I'm eighty-five or ninety-two, but… THANK GOD, I STILL HAVE MY DRIVER'S LICENSE.

* * *

The Four Stages of Life for a Man

1) You believe in Santa Claus.

2) You don't believe in Santa Claus.

3) You are Santa Claus.

4) You look like Santa Claus.

* * *

SENIORS ARE THE LEADING CARRIERS OF AIDS! HEARING AIDS, BAND AIDS, ROLL AIDS, MEDICAL AIDS, GOVERNMENT AIDS & MONETARY AIDS TO THEIR KIDS.

* * *

How Sex applies to Old Age:

    At twenty-thirty years tri-daily.

    At thirty-forty years tri-weekly.

    At forty-fifty years tri-weakly.

    At fifty-sixty years tri-oysters.

    At sixty-seventy years tri-Viagra.

    At seventy-eighty years tri-anything.

    At eighty-ninety years tri to remember.

* * *

To a man, the meaning of success depends on his age:

    At age four, success is not peeing in his pants.

    At age sixteen, success is getting a little.

    At age fifty, success is about career and family.

    At age sixty-five, success is getting a little.

    At age eighty, success is not peeing in his pants.

* * *

Why old men don't get hired...

Job Interview

Employer: What is your greatest weakness?

Old Man : Honesty.

Employer: I don't think honesty is a weakness.

Old Man : I don't really give a shit what you think.

* * *

The difference between grandmothers and grandfathers?

There was a loving grandfather who, every Saturday morning, would take his seven-year-old granddaughter for a drive in the car. One Saturday he didn't feel well, so he asked his wife to take her on the drive. When they returned, the little girl ran to her grandpa who asked, "Did you enjoy your ride with Grandma?" The girl replied, "Oh, yes, it was wonderful. We didn't see a single asshole, piece of crap, horse's ass, blind bastard, dipshit or son of a bitch anywhere we went!"

Brings a tear to your eye, doesn't it?

Part 11

Good Things About Getting Old...

Monday and Friday… are just another Saturday.

It's been years since the last time you gave a shit.

Being young is beautiful, but being old is comfortable.

People on Social Security rarely spread social diseases.

Realizing the old songs are best… because nobody sings them anymore.

As you get older, you realize that your investment in health insurance is finally beginning to pay off.

One good thing about getting old is when you borrow money from someone, you often forget who loaned it to you.

A man having a baby in his sixties is a good thing because he has to get up in the middle of the night anyway, so he may as well feed the baby.

When Grandma was a girl she didn't do the things girls do today. But then the grandmas then didn't do the things Grandma does today either.

* * *

Getting older has made me RICH: I have silver in my hair; gold in my teeth; crystals in my kidneys; sugar in my blood; lead in my butt ; iron in my arteries; and an inexhaustible supply of natural gas.

* * *

At eighteen, I wanted a girl with big boobs. I found her, but she had no passion. So at twenty-five, I found and dated a passionate girl, but she was too emotional, so I wanted a stable girl. At thirty, I found a stable girl, but she was too boring, so I decided I wanted an exciting girl. At forty, I found an exciting girl, but she was too much for me, so I decided I needed a girl who was ambitious. At fifty, I found an ambitious girl, and she took me for everything I had. I am older and wiser now… and I want a girl with big boobs.

* * *

New plan for seniors: You're a sick senior citizen, and the government says there's no nursing home available. Our plan gives anyone who is sixty-five years or older a gun and four bullets, and you're allowed to shoot four politicians. Of course, you'll be sent to prison where you'll get three meals a day, a roof over your head, and all the health care you need!

Need new teeth? Need glasses? No problem. Need a new hip, knees, kidney, lungs or heart? They're all covered. And your kids can come visit you as often as they do now. And who'll pay for all this? The same government that told you that they can't afford for you to go into a home. And because you're a prisoner, you don't have to pay income taxes anymore. Is this a great country or what!

* * *

Four games to play when you get older:

1) Sag, you're it.

2) Hide and go pee.

3) Musical Recliners.

4) Kick the bucket.

* * *

Old farts never die… they just run out of gas.

Old fisherman never die… they just smell that way.

Old mailmen never die… they just lose their zip.

Old rabbis never die… they just can't "cut" it anymore.

Old songwriters never die… they just decompose.

* * *

How do you get a sweet eighty-year-old lady to say "Fuck?"

Get another sweet old lady to yell, "BINGO!"

* * *

The first year a man gets married, his wife is a one-time gal. Once in the morning, once in the afternoon, once in the evening, once at night.

After ten years of marriage, his wife becomes a two-time gal. I'm too tired, it's too late, you're too drunk, it's too soft.

After forty years of marriage, his wife becomes a four-time gal. He approaches her and says, "How about it honey?" And she replies, "What For?"

* * *

So, I was visiting my granddaughter, and asked her if I could borrow a newspaper. She chuckled and replied, "This is the twenty-first century, Grandpa. People don't waste money on newspapers." She then handed me an iPad and said, "Here, use this." So I borrowed her iPad and I can tell you that fly never knew what hit him!

Part 12

Overheard in a Retirement Home with their oldest residents Jim & Sam

Jim: So what do you attribute your old age to?

Sam: The fact that I was born a long time ago.

* * *

Jim: I heard your sister is married to an archaeologist.

Sam: Yeah, she says it's great… because the older she gets… the more he's interested in her.

* * *

Jim: They say "things" improve with age.

Sam: Well, apparently my "thing" never heard that saying.

* * *

Jim: I went to the doctor's this morning for an exam.

Sam: What did your doctor say?

Jim: He said I was antique… I'm pretty sure he meant unique.

* * *

Jim: Did you know that even at my age, I can still make love five or six hours straight without stopping?

Sam: No kidding!

Jim: Yep, and even longer if I'm with someone.

* * *

Jim: Now that I'm in my eighties, women have to fall in love with me at first sight.

Sam: I know, because if they take a second look, you're finished.

* * *

Jim: My ninety-one-year-old brother Al is a true optimist.

Sam: Why do you say that?

Jim: Because he tells everyone he's in his *early* nineties.

Sam: That's nothing. My ninety-five-year-old cousin just got married and is looking for a home near a school.

* * *

Jim: I've got good news and bad news. Which do you wanna hear first?

Sam: Lemme hear the bad news.

Jim: My sister just died at the age of 102.

Sam: That *is* bad news. So what's the good news.

Jim: They were able to save the baby.

* * *

Sam: So what do you owe your long life to?

Jim: Mushrooms.

Sam: Really. Do you eat a lot of them?

Jim: No… I've never eaten them.

* * *

Jim: My eighty-six-year-old sister tried to commit suicide by putting a gun to her breast and pulling the trigger.

Sam: Did she die?

Jim: No, she survived, but shattered her knee.

* * *

Jim: My eighty-six-year-old sister was thinking of divorcing her husband of sixty years.

Sam: So what happened?

Jim: They decided to stay married for the sake of the parakeet.

* * *

Jim: My cousin Ted just turned 102 years old.

Sam: Wow. How do you think he's managed to live so long?

Jim: Well, he says it's because he quit smoking last year.

* * *

Jim: My seventy-seven-year-old neighbor Fred's forty-five-year-old wife is pregnant.

Sam: Ain't Fred kinda old to be getting someone pregnant?

Jim: Yeah. I'm pretty sure someone had it "in" for him.

* * *

Jim: Sam, if I ever come down with Alzheimer's, please do me a favor.

Sam: Sure Jim, anything.

Jim: Convince me that I'm Hugh Hefner.

* * *

Jim: When I had a kid, I didn't mind being a grandfather.

Sam: Me neither. What I didn't like was being married to a grandmother.

* * *

Jim: So what do you want your family to do if you're ever put on life support?

Sam: If I'm ever on life support, I want my family to unplug me… then plug me back in again to see if that works.

* * *

Jim: I haven't been able to sleep or eat since my wife Sue left me.

Sam: Sorry to hear that. You must have really loved her.

Jim: No… she took the bed and my teeth with her.

* * *

Jim: My wife asked me if, when I die, I want to be cremated or buried.

Sam: So what did you tell her?

Jim: I said, "Surprise me."

* * *

Jim: I just bought a new hearing aid. It cost $4,000 but it's state of the art. It's perfect.

Sam: Really, what kind is it?

Jim: Twelve thirty.

* * *

Jim: Some guys my age do it once a night, some guys twice a night, but I do it four or five times a night.

Sam: Maybe you shouldn't drink so much before going to bed.

* * *

Jim: There are three things that happen when you get old. First, you lose your memory.

Sam: And what are the other two?

Jim: I don't remember.

* * *

Jim: Even though I'm in my sixties, I still have a tremendous sex drive.

Sam: Are you serious?

Jim: Yeah… because my girlfriend lives over eighty miles from me.

* * *

Jim: Don't you think that, even though I'm old and grey, I still have a young looking body?

Sam: Yes, but mainly because of that diaper you're now wearing.

* * *

Jim: I finally found a way to keep my wife from biting her nails.

Sam: Really? What did you do?

Jim: I hid her teeth.

* * *

Jim: Hey Sam, Do you believe in the hereafter?

Sam: At my age, of course I believe in the hereafter. At least twice a day, I'll walk into a room and say to myself, "Now, what the hell did I come in hereafter?"

* * *

Part 13

The World's BEST "OLD" JOKES

Three old guys are out walking. The first old guy says, "Windy, isn't it?" The second old guy says, "No, it's Thursday!" The third old guy says, "So am I. Let's go get a beer."

* * *

A ninety-year-old man shows up at a brothel and asks a prostitute, "How Much?" She replies, "$200." The old man says, "You're putting me on." The hooker replies, "That's $50 extra."

* * *

Two old ladies are sitting in church. Suddenly, one lady leans over and whispers to the other, "My Butt is falling asleep." The other lady replies, "I know. I heard it snore three times."

* * *

An old man shows up at a brothel and asks the madam for sex. The madam says to the old guy, "How old are you?" The old man replies, "I'm ninety years old." "Ninety?" says the madam, "Don't you know you've had it?" "Oh" replies the old man, "How much do I owe you?"

* * *

A little old man shuffled slowly into an ice cream parlor and pulled himself carefully and painfully up onto a stool. After catching his breath, he ordered a banana split. The waitress looked at him with sympathy and asked, "Crushed nuts?" "No," The old geezer replied, "Arthritis."

* * *

Sue is on her death bed and gasps her last few words to her husband. With great difficulty, she whispers, "Bob, I have one final request. At my funeral, please ride in the first car with my mother." Bob replies, "All right… but it'll spoil my whole day."

* * *

Murray is on his death bed, and he says to his wife Sue, "Can you give me one last wish?" Sue says, "Anything you want." Murray says, "After I die, will you please marry Larry?" Sue says, "But I thought you hated Larry." With his last breath, Murray says, "I do."

* * *

Just before the funeral services for her husband, the undertaker approached the very elderly widow and asked, "How old was your husband?" "Ninety-eight," she replied, "A year older than me." "So you're ninety-seven," the undertaker commented. "Yes." She responded, The undertaker replied, "Hardly worth going home, is it?"

* * *

An old couple in their eighties are attending church services. About halfway through, the wife scribbles a note on a pad and passes it to her husband. It read, "I just let a silent fart, what should I do?" Her husband took the pad and wrote back…."We need to get new batteries for your hearing aid."

* * *

An old man goes to a doctor and says, "I have a problem." The Doctor asks, "What's wrong?" The old man replies… "I Can't PEE." The doctor asks, "How old are you?" The old man proudly sputters out… "I'm ninety-seven years old…" The doctor responds… "Well… You've peed enough."

* * *

Two elderly gentlemen from a retirement center were sitting on a bench under a tree when one turns to the other and says: "Murray, I'm eighty-three years old now, and I'm just full of aches and pains. I know you're about my age. How do you feel?" Murray says, "I feel just like a newborn baby." "Really!? Like a newborn baby!?" "Yep. No hair, no teeth, and I think I just wet my pants."

* * *

Murray, a ninety-year-old senior citizen, is driving down the freeway when his car phone suddenly rings. He answers, and it's his wife sounding worried, as she urgently warns him, "Murray, I just heard on the news that there's a car going the wrong way on Interstate 77." "Hell," says Murray, "It's not just one car. It's hundreds of them!"

* * *

A college student saw an old man sitting on a park bench sobbing and asked him "What's wrong?" The elderly man responded, "Last weekend I married a beautiful twenty-five-year-old woman with a gorgeous body who loves sex with older men." The student grinned and said, "What's wrong with that?" And the old man replied, "I forgot where I live!"

* * *

Three old ladies are sitting on a park bench, when a flasher approaches them, opens his raincoat and flashes them… The first lady, in her sixties, has a stroke… The second old lady, in her seventies, also has a stroke… The third old lady, in her eighties, doesn't have a stroke… because she is really old… and can't reach that far.

* * *

An old man goes to the doctor for an exam. After the exam, the doctor tells him, "I've got bad news and worse news." The man says, "Okay, gimme the bad news first." The doctor says, "You've got AIDS." The old man says, "Oh no…So, what's the worse news?" The doctor replies, "You've got Alzheimer's"… After a moment, the old guy replies "Well… at least I don't have AIDS."

* * *

A senior citizen said to his eighty-year-old buddy: "So I hear you're getting married?" "Yep!" "Do I know her?" "Nope!" "This woman, is she good looking?" "Not really." "Is she a good cook?" "Naw, she can't cook too well." "Does she have lots of money?" "Nope! Poor as a church mouse." "Well, then, is she good in bed?" "I don't know." "Why in the world do you want to marry her then?" "Because she can still drive!"

* * *

A ninety-year-old man is walking on the beach when he hears a voice and sees a tiny frog. It says, "Hey Mister, if you kiss me I'll turn into a beautiful woman and your wishes will be my commands forever." He takes the frog puts it in his pocket and walks away. The frog says "Hey what are ya doing? Don't ya want to kiss me?" The old man says, "Hell no! At my age, a talking frog is worth a whole lot more to me."

* * *

An older Jewish woman meets a man at a party. She asks him. "How long have you been in town?" He says, "About a month. I was gone for a few years." "Really," she replies, "Where were you? In Europe?" "No," he says, "I was in Prison." "Really," she continues, "And why were you in Prison?" He responds,

"For killing my wife with an axe."… She suddenly smiles and replies "Sooooooo…you're SINGLE."

* * *

The irate elderly woman called the newspaper office and loudly demanded to know where her Sunday edition was. "Madam," said the newspaper employee, "today is Saturday. The Sunday paper is not delivered until tomorrow, on SUNDAY." There was quite a long pause on the other end of the phone, followed by a ray of recognition as the woman was heard to mutter… "Well, shit, that explains why no one was at church either."

* * *

Murray, an eighty-two-year-old man, went to the doctor to get a physical. A few days later, the doctor saw Murray walking down the street with a gorgeous young woman on his arm. A couple of days later, the doctor spoke to Murray and said, "You're really doing great, aren't you?" Murray replied, "Just doing what you said, Doc: 'Get a hot mamma and be cheerful." The doctor said, "I didn't say that. I said, 'You've got a heart murmur—be careful.'"

* * *

Joey is out with his friends and stops by his grandmother's house for a visit. There's a bowl of peanuts on the coffee table. So Joey and his friends start snacking on them. When they're ready to leave, his friends say, "Nice to meet you, ma'am, And thank you for the peanuts." Grandma replies, "You're welcome. I'm glad you ate them all. Ever since I lost my dentures, all I can do is suck the chocolate off 'em."

* * *

An older lady has two pet monkeys she has been raising for years. One is male and one is female. Suddenly the male monkey gets sick and dies. A couple of days later, the female monkey misses its mate so much, it also dies of a broken heart. Wishing to keep them, the lady takes them to a taxidermist who asks her, "Do you want them mounted?" The old lady thinks for a moment then replies, "Oh, no…just have them holding hands."

* * *

Three old guys are talking. The first guy, seventy-six, says, "My hearing is going. When I ask my wife for sex, I can't hear if she said yes or no…" The second guy, eighty-five, says, "Well my eyesight is going. If my wife comes out of the bathroom naked, I can't see a thing.." The third guy, ninety-three, says, "I'm worse than you guys. Last night, when my wife was asleep, I shook her and said 'let's have sex.' She yelled, "But we just had sex twenty minutes ago." It's horrible. My frickin' memory is going."

* * *

An old couple in their nineties are in divorce court. The judge asks "How long have you two been married?" The ninety-four-year-old husband replies, "Seventy-five years." The judge says, "And when did you two begin having problems in your marriage?"

The ninety-two-year-old wife says, "About seventy years ago." The shocked judge says, "Seventy years ago? Well, why did you wait so long to apply for a divorce?" The old couple replied, "Because we wanted to wait until all the kids had died."

* * *

At the World Series, a man sees a seat next to him is empty. He asks his older neighbor if he knows why? The old man says, "The seat is mine, and I was supposed to come with my wife but she passed away. This is the first World Series we haven't been to together since we married in 1962." "That's terrible," says the man, "but couldn't you find someone, a friend, relative, or neighbor to take the seat?" The man replies, "Not really. They're all at the funeral."

* * *

Eighty-nine-year-old Murray says to his wife, "I'm giving up golf. My eyes are so bad I can't see where I hit the ball." His wife says, "Take my brother Bob with you." "Why?" says Murray, "Bob is ninety." "He may be ninety," says his wife, "but his eyesight is perfect." So the next day, Murray takes ninety-year-old Bob golfing. Murray swings, then says to Bob "Did you see the ball?" "Of course." says Bob, "I have perfect eyesight." Murray asks, "Where did it go?" Bob replies, "I don't remember."

* * *

In a park, Old Man Murray is sitting on a bench when a teenager with spiked yellow, green, and orange hair sits next to him. The teen has black make-up around his eyes and wears bright, neon colored clothes. The old man stares at him. The teen notices and says, "What's the matter old man? Haven't you ever done anything wild in your life?" The old man replies, "Yes, I once got drunk and fucked a parrot… and I was just wondering if you were my son?"

* * *

An old man enters a church, goes to confession, and says to the priest, "Father, I'm eighty years old, been married fifty years, and I've been having sex with a nineteen-year-old girlfriend twice a day for over three months." The priest says, "You need to say the rosary fifty times." The old man replies "For what? I'm not Catholic. I'm Jewish." The priest says, "Jewish? Then why are you telling me this?" The old man replies, "Are you kidding? I'm eighty, and I'm screwing a nineteen-year-old. I'm telling *everyone*."

* * *

An old lady tells her doctor, "I have awful gas, but it's completely silent and it doesn't smell." The doctor examines her, gives her some pills, and tells her to take one every day, and return in a week. The lady returns, and when the doctor asks if her problem is better, she says, "I don't know what you gave me but now my gas smells terrible!" The doctor replies "Well now that we've got your sinuses cleared up, let's work on your hearing!"

* * *

Old Man Murray was recently moved to a new retirement home. One day, he is sitting outside, when suddenly he begins to lean over to the left. A nurse sees him, rushes over, and props him up. This happens several times, but each time he leans over, the nurse is there to straighten him out. The next day, Murray's son stops by and asks how he likes the new home. Murray replies, "The food's okay, the rooms are nice, but the damn nurse won't let me fart."

* * *

Three men in their eighties are in a retirement home. The first man says, "Getting old is a bitch. I have to get up three or four times a night to pee." The second man says, "For me it's worse. I can't shit sometimes for a week." The third man says, "I'm older than both of you, and every morning I pee at exactly seven and take a shit at exactly eight." The other two men say, "You are so lucky." The third man replies, "Not really. I don't wake up until nine."

* * *

A couple in their sixties are on their fortieth anniversary in Hawaii. As they both sit naked at breakfast after a night of celebration, the wife stares at her husband and says, "I can't believe it, but after forty years of marriage, I look at you and you still make my nipples tingle." The husband replies, "Thanks for the compliment dear, but the real reason is because your left breast is in your coffee and your right one is in your oatmeal."

* * *

Sixty-year-old Murray is at his doctor's for the results of an examination. The doctor says, "I've got terrible news. I don't know how it happened but we got your test results mixed up with someone else. Either you've got Alzheimer's or AIDS." A shocked Murray replies, "Oh my God. That's terrible. What should I do?" The doctor replies, "Well, after you leave my office, if you find your way home... Don't fuck your wife."

* * *

An old couple, married sixty years, decided to go on a second honeymoon and went to the same hotel they had gone to sixty years earlier. That night after dinner, she slipped into bed in a skimpy nightgown while he went to the bathroom. After fifteen minutes, she got worried and went into the bathroom to check up on him and found him struggling to put on a condom. "Why are you putting on a condom?" she asked, "I'm eighty-two... I can't get pregnant." "I know," he said, "but you know how dampness affects my arthritis."

* * *

An elderly gentleman had serious hearing problems for a number of years. He went to the doctor, and the doctor was able to have him fitted for a set of hearing aids that allowed the gentleman to hear 100 percent. The elderly gentleman went back in a month to the doctor, and the doctor said, "Your hearing is perfect. Your family must be really pleased that you can hear again." The gentleman replied, "Oh, I haven't told my family yet. I just sit around and listen to the conversations. I've changed my will three times!"

* * *

Two older ladies in their eighties, who had been friends for decades, continued their friendship by playing cards once a week. One day, they were playing, when one looked at the other and said, "Now, don't get mad at me. I know we've been friends a long time but I just can't think of your name. I've thought and thought but can't remember it. Please tell me what your name is?" Her friend stared at her for several minutes then finally said, "How soon do you need to know?"

* * *

A group of Americans was traveling by tour bus through Holland. As they stopped at a cheese farm, a guide led them through the process of cheese making, explaining that goat's milk was used. She showed them a hillside where many goats were grazing. "These," she explained, "are the older goats put out to pasture when they no longer produce." She then asked, "What do you do in America with your old goats?" One of the old guys replied, "They send us on bus tours!"

* * *

A doctor gives an old man a jar and asks him to bring back a semen sample. The old man returns with an empty jar and says, "Sorry doc, I tried with my right and left hand and nothing. My wife tried with both hands, then her mouth with her teeth in and out and again, nothing. We asked the lady next door who tried with her armpit and between her knees and nothing. The surprised doctor says, "You asked your neighbor?" The old man replies, "Yep… and none of us could get that damn jar open."

* * *

A couple is married forty years when the wife suddenly dies. After the funeral, the pallbearers are carrying the casket out when they accidentally bump into a wall, jarring the casket. They hear a faint moan, open the casket, and find the wife is actually alive. She lives for ten more years and then dies again. A funeral is held, and once again, the pallbearers are carrying out the casket. As they are walking, the husband yells to the pallbearers… "Watch out for that wall!"

* * *

An eighty-year-old lady was marrying for the fourth time. A newspaper asked if she wouldn't mind talking about her husbands and what they did for a living. She smiled and said, "My first husband was a banker, my second was a circus ringmaster, my third was a preacher, and my fourth and current husband is a funeral director. When asked why the four men had such diverse careers, she explained, "I married one for the money, two for the show, three to get ready and four to go."

* * *

At the end of Sunday service, the minister asked the congregation, "How many of you have forgiven your enemies?" All responded, except one old lady. "Are you not willing to forgive your enemies?" "I don't have any," she replied. "Madam, that is unusual. How old are you?" asked the minister. "Ninety-eight," she said, and the congregation applauded. The minister continued, "Madam would you please tell us how a person can live ninety-eight years and not have any enemies?" The old lady replied, "I outlived the bitches."

* * *

A husband and wife in their sixties were celebrating their fortieth wedding anniversary at the beach. They stumbled upon a bottle, and when they picked it up, a genie suddenly appeared, offering each of them one wish. The wife wished for a trip around the world with her husband, and whooooosshhh… instantly she had airline and cruise tickets appear in her hands. Her husband thought for a minute, then wished for a woman who was thirty years younger than he was… and instantly… he turned ninety!!!

* * *

After the eighty-three-year-old lady finished her annual physical examination, the doctor said, "You are in fine shape for your age, Maxine, but tell me, do you still have intercourse?" "Just a minute, I'll have to ask my husband," she said. She stepped out into the crowded reception room and yelled out loud: "Henry, do we still have intercourse ?" And there was a hush… You could hear a pin drop. He answered impatiently, "If I told you once, Maxine, I told you a hundred times .... What we have is...Blue Cross!!"

* * *

In a retirement home, seventy-nine-year-old Fran approaches eighty-nine-year-old Murray and says, "I bet I can tell you how old you are." Murray replies, "Oh yeah, how old am I?" Fran says, "Show me your ass and I'll tell you how old you are." So Murray drops his pants and shows her his naked ass. Fran looks his ass over and squeezes the cheeks of his butt, then says, "You're eighty-nine." A surprised Murray replies, "You're right. How did you know that?" Fran responds, "You told me this morning at breakfast."

* * *

A man asks his wife what she wants for her sixtieth birthday. She says, "I'd like to be six again." On her birthday morning, he feeds her Lucky Charms then takes her to Disneyland and puts her on every ride. Afterward, it's off to McDonald's where he orders her a Happy Meal and then takes her to a kid's movie! That night, she is exhausted and tired as he says, "Well, what was it like being six again?" She looks at him angrily and replies "I meant my dress size, you fucking idiot."

* * *

On a windy day, an old lady at a bus stop is holding her hat tightly in her hands so it won't blow away. A man approaches and says, "Pardon me, but your dress is blowing up in the wind" "Yes, I know," says the lady. "I need both hands to hold onto my hat."

The man says, "You should know you are not wearing panties and your privates are exposed!" The woman looks down and replies, "Sir, anything you see down there is eighty-five years old. I just bought this hat yesterday!"

* * *

An old couple are at the doctor's office. The doctor asks them if there are any concerns they'd like to discuss? The old man says, "Lately when I have sex with my wife, I've noticed that after the first time I'm usually hot and sweaty and after the second time I'm cold and chilly." The doctor replies. "Mmmm, I've never heard of this." The wife jumps in and says, "The reason he's hot and sweaty after the first time we have sex, and cold and chilly after the second time we have sex is because the first time is usually in July and the second time is usually in December!"

* * *

An older couple celebrating their fiftieth anniversary is nestled in front of a fireplace having a glass of wine when the woman turns to the man and says, "I miss your kisses." That said, he reached over and kissed her long and sweet. She smiled and said, "And I miss when you would hold my hand in yours." He picked up her hand and held it gently in his. "And I miss when you used to bite me on the back of the neck." He suddenly got up and walked out of the room. She shouted to him, "Where are you going?" He answered, "To get my teeth."

* * *

Bob is on his deathbed as his wife Sue holds his hand. He looks up and whispers, "My darling Sue, I'm dying and I don't have much time left but I have to talk. I have something I must confess to you." Sue replies, "There's nothing to confess, go to sleep." Bob persists, "No, I must die in peace." He gathers his strength and continues, "Sue, I'm so sorry, but I slept with your sister and your best friend." Sue replies softly, "Hush now, I know all about it." Bob is shocked as he responds, "You do?" Sue replies, "Of course. Why do you think I poisoned you?"

* * *

An old man at a retirement home was walking around holding onto his groin area. A young nurse stopped him and said "Why are you doing that?" The old guy looked up and replied sadly, "My penis died today." "Oh that's terrible!" replied the understanding nurse. The next day the same old man was again walking around, and this time, his zipper was down and his penis was hanging outside of his pants. The same nurse spots him and says, "What are you doing? I thought your penis died yesterday." The old man replies, "It did. Today is the viewing."

* * *

A grandson asks his grandpa what sex is like. Grandpa says, "Well when you first get married, you want it all the time. Later on, sex tapers off and you have it maybe once or twice a week. As you get older you have sex maybe once a month. Then when you get really old, you're lucky to have it once a year. Finally, when you reach our age, you just have oral sex." The grandson replies, confused, "Oral sex?" And Grandpa says, "Yep… Grandma goes in her bedroom and I go in my bedroom and she yells "fuck you," and I holler back "fuck you too."

* * *

A man came to visit his grandparents and noticed his grandfather sitting on the porch in the rocking chair wearing only a shirt and nothing on from the waist down. "Grandpa, what are you doing? Your weenie is out in the wind for everyone to see!" he exclaimed. The old man looked off in the distance without answering. "Grandpa, what are you doing sitting out here with nothing on below the waist?" he asked again. The old man slowly looked at him and said, "Well, last week I sat out here with no shirt on and I got a stiff neck. This is your grandma's idea."

* * *

A lonely older lady goes to a hotel on her sixtieth birthday. She thinks, "I'll call one of those ads in the phone books for male escorts and massages." She finds one that sounds perfect, figuring *why not, nobody will know*. She dials, and a sexy sounding man says, "Hello may I help you?" She says, "I hear you give massages. Please come to my hotel room and give me one. Wait, the truth is I want sex. I want it hot, and bring toys, everything you've got." The voice on the other end says, "Sounds great, but you need to press nine for an outside line."

* * *

A couple in their sixties go to a sex therapist's office and ask how much to watch them have sex. The doctor says $75, and they agree. This happens for months. The couple has sex with no problems, pay the doctor, and leave. Finally, after six months, the doc says, "I'm sorry but what are you trying to find out?" The man says, "Nothing! She's married so we can't go to her house. I'm married and we can't go to my house. The Holiday Inn charges $159. The Hilton charges $198. We do it here for $75 and Medicare pays $65 of it, leaving me a net cost of $10."

* * *

Murray, an eighty-year-old man tells his doctor that he's going to marry a twenty-four-year-old woman. His concerned doctor says, "At your age this could have serious consequences. You might want to consider taking in a young, energetic roommate." The old guy tells the doctor that he will consider it. A year later, Murray now eighty-one, revisits his doctor, who asks, "And how is married life?" Murray replies, "Wonderful… and I'm happy to say that my young wife is pregnant." The doctor says, "Congratulations… and did you take my advice about acquiring a younger roommate?" "Yes I did," replied Murray… "And she's pregnant too…"

* * *

An old widow placed an ad: *HUSBAND WANTED: MUST BE IN MY AGE GROUP, MUST NOT BEAT ME, MUST NOT RUN AROUND, AND MUST BE GOOD IN BED!* Next day, she heard a knock, opened the door to see a grey-haired man in a wheelchair with no arms or legs. The old lady said, "You're not asking me to consider you? You have no legs!" The old man smiled, "Therefore I can't run around on you!" She continued, "And no arms either!" Again, he smiled, "Therefore I can't beat you!" She then asked, "Are you still good in bed?" The old man smiled and said, "Rang the doorbell didn't I?"

* * *

Bob and Sue, both ninety-one, met at a singles club and discovered they liked each other. After weeks of meeting for coffee, Bob asked Sue out for dinner, and to his delight, she accepted. They dined at a romantic restaurant and, despite their age, ended up at his place for an after-dinner drink. Things continued and Sue soon joined Bob for an enjoyable roll in the hay. As they were basking in the after-glow of sex, Bob said to her, "If I'd known you were a virgin, I'd have been gentler." Sue replied, "If I'd known you could still do it, I'd have taken off my pantyhose."

* * *

An old man at a party sees a woman with perfect breasts, and after a few drinks, he saunters over to her and asks, "Could I bite your breasts for $100?" The woman replies, "Are you nuts?" The old man asks again, "Could I bite them for $1,000?" Again the woman replies, "NO, not interested." The old man continues, "Could I bite them just once for $10,000?" She thinks and says "$10,000, OK, bite them just once," and she removes her blouse. Immediately, the old man caresses and fondles them, kisses and licks them but doesn't bite them. The woman, annoyed, asks, "Are you gonna bite them or not?" "Nah," says the old man. "Costs too much!"

* * *

An elderly couple had dinner at another couple's house, and after eating, the wives left the table and went to the kitchen. The two old guys were talking, and one said, "Last night we went to a new restaurant which was great. I would recommend it highly." The other man said, "What's the name of the restaurant?" The first man replied, "Mmmm, I forgot. Lemme think." After thinking hard, he asked, "What's the name of that flower you give to someone you love? You know… The one that's red and has thorns." The second man said, "Do you mean a rose?" "Yes, that's the one," replied the first man. He then turned towards the kitchen and yelled, "Rose, what's the name of that restaurant we went to last night?"

* * *

The seventy-five-year-old boss walked into the office one morning, not knowing his zipper was down and his fly area wide open. His assistant walked up to him and said, "This morning when you left your house, did you close your garage door?" The boss told her he knew he'd closed the garage door and walked into his office puzzled by the question. As he finished his paperwork, he suddenly noticed his fly was open and zipped it up. He then understood his assistant's question about his garage door. He headed out for a cup of coffee and paused by her desk to ask, "When my garage door was open, did you see my Hummer parked in there?" She smiled and said, "No, I didn't. All I saw was an old minivan with two flat tires."

* * *

Three sisters ages ninety-one, ninety-three, and ninety-five live together in the same house. One night, the ninety-five-year-old draws a bath. She puts her foot in, then pauses. She yells out to her sisters, "Was I getting in the bath or getting out of the bath?" The ninety-three-year-old sister yells back, "I don't know. I'll come up and see." She starts up the stairs, then pauses and yells, "Was I going up the stairs or down the stairs?" The ninety-one-year-old, having tea at the kitchen table, hears them and says to herself, *I sure hope I never get that forgetful.* Then, for good measure, she taps on the table and says, "Knock on wood." She then yells out, "I'll be there in a minute as soon as I see who's at the door."

* * *

Grandpa was fishing with his grandson Billy and he lit up a cigarette. "Grandpa," asked Billy, "Can I try one of your cigarettes?" "Can you touch your asshole with you penis?" asked Grandpa. "No," said Billy. "Then you're not old enough for cigarettes." Grandpa then opened a beer. "Grandpa, can I try some of your beer?" asked Billy. "Can you touch your asshole with your penis?" Grandpa asked again. "No," replied Billy. "Then you're not old enough for beer." Later,

Billy removed cookies from his pocket. "Those look good," said Grandpa, "Can I have one of your cookies?" "Can you touch your asshole with your penis?" asked Billy. "I sure can." said Grandpa. Billy replied, "Then go fuck yourself, these are my cookies."

* * *

An old guy is sent by his doctor to a urologist. When he arrives, he discovers the urologist is a pretty female. She says to him, "I'm going to check your prostate, but this new procedure is a little different from what you're used to. I want you to lie on your right side, bend your knees, and while I check your prostate, take a deep breath and say… ninety-nine." The old guy obeys and says, "ninety-nine." The doctor says, "Now turn over on your left side and again, while I repeat the check, take a deep breath and say… ninety-nine." Again, the old guy says, "ninety-nine." She says, "Very good. Now I want you to lie on your back with your knees raised slightly. I'm going to check your prostate with one hand and with the other hand I'm going to hold your penis to keep it out of the way. Now take a deep breath and say …ninety-nine." The old guy says, "One…two… three…"

* * *

Upon hearing that her elderly grandfather had passed away, Sue went to their house to visit her ninety-five-year-old grandmother and comfort her. When she asked how her grandpa had died, her grandmother replied, "He had a heart attack while we were making love on Sunday morning." Shocked, Sue told her grandmother that two people nearly 100 years old having sex would surely be asking for trouble. "Oh no, my dear," replied Grandma. "Years ago realizing our advanced age, we figured out the best time to have sex was when the church bells would start to ring. It was just the right rhythm. Nice and slow. Nothing too strenuous, simply in on the ding and out on the dong." She paused to wipe away a tear and continued, "He'd still be alive if that fucking ice cream truck hadn't come along."

* * *

Sixty-year-old Bob comes home drunk, falls asleep with his wife Sue, then hours later awakes and finds himself in front of St. Peter, who says "Bob, you just died in your sleep." Bob, shocked says, "NO! Send me back!" St Peter says, "Okay I can do that but you can only go back as a chicken." Bob says, "Fine. Whatever. I'll be a chicken but I want to go back." Next thing, Bob is a chicken, and suddenly he sees a rooster who says, "How'ya doing?" Bob replies, "Okay but I have this feeling I'm gonna explode!" The rooster says, "You're ovulating. You're gonna lay an egg. Relax and let it happen." Bob tries to relax and suddenly out pops an egg! Bob is overcome with motherhood and lays another egg. Then, as he's about to lay a third egg, he feels a smack on his head and hears his wife Sue say, "Bob, Wake Up! You just shit in the bed!"

* * *

Two old ladies, Jan and Sue, living in a retirement home are chatting. Jan says, "That nice older gentleman Bill Baxter just asked me out for a date." Sue says, "Well he asked me out last week and I went out with him." Jan says, "Really and what was he like?" Sue replies, "Well I went out and bought a new dress and he picked me up promptly at eight like he said he would. He was dressed like a gentleman and brought me flowers. Then he took me downstairs with a Limo waiting and we went out for dinner. We dined on lobster and champagne, and after went to a marvelous play. Let me tell you, I really enjoyed it all and everything was great, but when we returned to my place, he turned into an animal, tearing off my new dress and had his way with me three times." "Oh my!" said Jan, "So you're saying I shouldn't go with him?" "No," replied Sue, "I'm just saying, wear an old dress."

* * *

A nurse was making her rounds in a nursing home. She came across an open door, looked in, and saw eighty-eight-year-old Murray sitting up in bed pretending to drive. She asked, "Murray, what are you doing?" Murray replied, "I'm driving to Las Vegas." The nurse smiled and continued on her rounds. The next night as she walked past Murray's room she saw the same thing and again asked, "Murray, what are you doing?" Murray replied, "I'm driving to Las Vegas. It's a two day trip you know!" The nurse smiled and carried on with her rounds. Five minutes later, she came across another open door, looked in and saw Murray's best friend, eighty-six-year-old Bob pretending to dance with someone. She asked, "Bob, what are you doing?" Bob replied, "I'm dancing with Murray's wife. He's gone to Vegas for a couple of days."

* * *

Two old Jews, Sid and Al, are sitting in a Cuban restaurant. Sid asks Al, "Do you know if there are any Jews in Cuba?" Al replies, "I don't know, let's ask our waiter." When the waiter arrives, Al asks, "Are there any Cuban Jews?" The waiter says, "I don't know, Señor, I ask the cooks." He returns a minute later and says, "No, Señor, the cook say no Cuban Jews." Al isn't satisfied and asks, "Are you absolutely sure?" The waiter, realizing he is dealing with 'Gringos,' replies, "I check once again, Señor." While the waiter is away, Sid says, "I find it hard to believe that there are no Jews in Cuba. Our people are scattered everywhere." The waiter returns and says, "Señor, the cook say there is no Cuban Jews." Al asks, "Are you sure? I just can't believe there are no Cuban Jews." The exasperated waiter says, "Señor, I ask EVERYONE... All we have is orange Jews, prune Jews and tomato Jews."

* * *

Bob and Sue, two math teachers who had been married for forty years, took a vacation every year together. However, this year they discussed having separate vacations. They agreed that the time was right, so Bob went to Hawaii and Sue to Cancun. After a week, Sue called Bob and asked how it was going? "Just great." Bob replied, "To be honest, I've spent time with the maid I met here. She's blonde, only twenty, and we've been enjoying each other's company. How about you?" Sue answered. "I'm having a great time. Met this young nineteen-year-old surfer boy and we've been seeing a lot of each other. And as a math teacher I've learned more about my profession." Bob replied, "Really. How so?" Sue answered, "Well, I learned that nineteen goes into sixty more than sixty-five goes into twenty."

* * *

A sixty-year-old man went to the doctor for a checkup. The doctor said, "You're in great shape. You have the body of a thirty-five-year-old. How old was your father when he died?" The sixty-year-old man replied, "Did I say he was dead?" The surprised doctor asked, "How old is he and is he active?" The sixty-year-old said, "He's eighty-two and still goes skiing all winter and surfs all summer." The shocked doctor asked, "So how old was your grandfather when he died?" The sixty-year-old responded, "Did I say he was dead?" The doctor replied, "You mean to say you're sixty and both your father and grandfather are alive? Is your grandfather still active?" The sixty-year-old said, "He also still goes skiing during the winter and surfs all summer. Not only that, my grandfather is now 106 and he's getting married next week." The astonished doctor said, "Why on earth would your 106-year-old grandfather want to get married?" The sixty-year-old replied, "Did I say he wanted to?"

* * *

A little old lady was walking down the street dragging two large plastic garbage bags. One of the bags was ripped and $20 bills kept falling out. Noticing this, a cop stopped her and said, "Ma'am, there are $20 bills falling out of that bag." "Oh, really? Darn it!" said the old lady. "I'd better go and see if I can find them. Thanks, Officer." The cop said, "Where did you get all that money? You didn't steal it, did you?" "Oh, no," said the old lady. "My back yard is next to a golf course. A lot of golfers come and pee through a knot hole in my fence into my flower garden. It used to really tick me off, then I thought, why not make the best of it? So, now, I stand by the knot hole with my hedge clippers. Every time some guy sticks his thing through my fence, I grab hold of it and say, "O.K., buddy! Give me $20, or off it comes." "Really?" said the cop laughing, "And what's in the other bag?" The lady replied, "Not everybody pays."

* * *

Benny is lying in bed dying. His wife of fifty years, Becky, is holding his hand. Benny opens his eyes, sees her and says, "Becky, look at you holding my hand as I lay here dying. For as long as I can remember, you were always holding my hand. Do you remember during the war when we were captured by the Nazis, you were holding my hand. And after the war, we ate out of garbage cans to survive and you were there holding my hand. And then we came to America and worked eighteen hours a day for years until we saved enough money to buy a house, then a month later it burned down and you were there holding my hand." Tears well up in Becky's eyes as Benny continues, "Then we had to move in with relatives for years and we fought with them constantly but you were always there holding my hand. And now I find out I am dying and here you are still holding my hand. You know what I think, Becky? Becky bends over and whispers. "No, what do you think, Benny?" Benny replies "I think you're a fucking jinx."

* * *

Bob and Sue, both eighty-five, had been married sixty years, and were in good health, largely due to Sue's insistence on healthy food and exercise. One day, their good health didn't help when they were in a plane crash and sent to Heaven. At the pearly gates, St. Peter took them to a mansion with a fully stocked kitchen and a waterfall in the master bath. Bob asked how much all this was going to cost. "Why, nothing," Peter replied, "This is Heaven." Bob looked out the window and saw a championship golf course. "What are the greens fees?" Bob asked. St. Peter replied, "Don't be ridiculous. You play for free, every day." Next they went to the clubhouse and saw a lavish buffet. "Don't even ask," said St. Peter to Bob. "It's all free. You can eat and drink as much as you like and you'll never get fat or sick. This is Heaven!" "No gym to work out at?" asked Bob. "Nope." "No testing my sugar or blood pressure or…" "Never again," said St Peter. Bob glared at Sue and said, "You and your frickin' Bran Flakes. We could have been here ten years ago."

* * *

A couple in their nineties are both having problems remembering things. During a checkup, the doctor tells them that they're physically okay but they might want to start writing things down to help them remember. Later that night, while watching TV, the old man gets up from his chair. "Want anything while I'm in the kitchen?" he asks. "Will you get me a bowl of ice cream?" "Sure." "Don't you think you should write it down so you can remember it?" she asks. "No, I can remember it." "Well, I'd like some strawberries on top too. Maybe you should write it down, so as not to forget it?" He says, "I can remember that. You want a bowl of ice cream with strawberries." "I'd also like whipped cream. I'm certain you'll forget that, write it down?" she asks. Irritated, he says, "I don't need to write it down, I can remember it! Ice cream with strawberries and whipped cream—I got it, for goodness sake!" Then he toddles into the kitchen. After about twenty minutes, the old man returns from the kitchen and hands his wife a plate of bacon and eggs. She stares at the plate for a moment and, irritated, says, "Where's my toast ?"

* * *

Part 14

LIFE IS REALLY WONDERFUL
Don't Miss It If Cou Can...

And Remember:

Everyone dies… but not everyone lives.

Don't just enjoy each day… enjoy each minute.

The best thing to save for old age… is yourself.

Live every day like it was your last… and eventually, it will be.

If you haven't grown up by age fifty… then you don't have to.

You're only here for a short time, so make it a good time.

Life is much more enjoyable when you reach the age when you don't give a shit.

In life, you can either scream at every bump or you can just throw your hands in the air and enjoy the ride.

THE END

www.ingramcontent.com/pod-product-compliance
Lightning Source LLC
Chambersburg PA
CBHW070938160426
43193CB00011B/1734